Central Asia and Its Asian Neighbors

Security and Commerce at the Crossroads

Rollie Lal

Prepared for the United States Air Force

 PROJECT AIR FORCE

The research described in this report was sponsored by the United States Air Force under Contract F49642-01-C-0003. Further information may be obtained from the Strategic Planning Division, Directorate of Plans, Hq USAF.

Library of Congress Cataloging-in-Publication Data

Lal, Rollie.
  Central Asia and its Asian neighbors : security and commerce at the crossroads / Rollie Lal.
    p. cm.
  "MG-440."
  Includes bibliographical references.
  ISBN 0-8330-3878-8 (pbk. : alk. paper)
    1. Asia, Central—Relations—Asia. 2. Asia—Relations—Asia, Central. 3. Asian cooperation. 4. Asia—Relations—United States. 5. United States—Relations—Asia. I. Title.

  DS33.4.A783L35 2006
  327.7305—dc22

                                                                    2005031207

The RAND Corporation is a nonprofit research organization providing objective analysis and effective solutions that address the challenges facing the public and private sectors around the world. RAND's publications do not necessarily reflect the opinions of its research clients and sponsors.

RAND® is a registered trademark.

Cover photograph by Rollie Lal

Published 2006 by the RAND Corporation
1776 Main Street, P.O. Box 2138, Santa Monica, CA 90407-2138
1200 South Hayes Street, Arlington, VA 22202-5050
4570 Fifth Avenue, Suite 600, Pittsburgh, PA 15213
RAND URL: http://www.rand.org/
To order RAND documents or to obtain additional information, contact
Distribution Services: Telephone: (310) 451-7002;
Fax: (310) 451-6915; Email: order@rand.org

Central Asia

Preface

The countries of Central Asia are greatly influenced by their Asian neighbors. Much analysis has been put forth on the issue of the relations between the Central Asian states and Russia, but the countries to the south and east, including China, Iran, Afghanistan, India, and Pakistan, also have a powerful but less understood effect on the Central Asian states' security and economic interests.[1]

This monograph assesses the mutual interests of the Central Asian states and their Asian neighbors, and considers the implications of these interests for the United States. It also looks at the role of relations between the states of the region in this context, and at the role of multinational organizations such as the Shanghai Cooperation Organization (SCO). This monograph should be of interest to policymakers and analysts involved in international security and U.S. foreign policy.

The analysis in this monograph is informed by a yearlong research effort, which included travel to the region and extensive interviews with U.S., regional, and global specialists; government officials; and others. It involved a multidisciplinary team of researchers who sought to combine their understanding of politics, economics, and military strategic analysis to bring fresh perspectives to the questions at hand.

This monograph is one of several reporting the results of the research effort. Other documents address political structures and par-

---

[1] See Burghart and Sabonis-Helf (2004); Oliker and Shlapak (2005).

ticipation; religion, ethnicity, and clans; and economic development. In addition, a broad overview monograph, *U.S. Interests in Central Asia: Policy Priorities and Military Roles*, draws on the material in all of these assessments to define future requirements and approaches to the region. Each of these will be published separately, forthcoming from RAND.

The research reported here was sponsored by AF/XOX and conducted within the Strategy and Doctrine Program of RAND Project AIR FORCE. Comments are welcome and may be directed to the authors and to Andrew Hoehn, director of Project AIR FORCE's (PAF's) Strategy and Doctrine Program. Until late 2003, the then-director of PAF's Strategy and Doctrine program, Dr. Edward Harshberger, provided leadership and support. Research for this report was completed in May 2005.

RAND Project AIR FORCE

RAND Project AIR FORCE (PAF), a division of the RAND Corporation, is the U.S. Air Force's federally funded research and development center for studies and analyses. PAF provides the Air Force with independent analyses of policy alternatives affecting the development, employment, combat readiness, and support of current and future aerospace forces. Research is conducted in four programs: Aerospace Force Development; Manpower, Personnel, and Training; Resource Management; and Strategy and Doctrine.

Additional information about PAF is available on our web site at http://www.rand.org/paf.

Contents

Summary

The Asian states neighboring Central Asia have historic links and strong interests in the region. China, Iran, Afghanistan, India, and Pakistan are critical players in the security and economic issues that will determine the future of Central Asia and affect U.S. interests in the region. All of these states are of importance to the United States, whether due to the war on terrorism, economic ties, arms control, nonproliferation, or other reasons. China, Iran, and India have all aggressively sought to build trade ties to and through Central Asia, and China and India have also invigorated security cooperation. But regional states are concerned about the situation in Afghanistan, which they fear might lead to a spillover of conflict onto their soil, and they also fear the possibility of Pakistani activity and influence, which has led them to keep that state at arm's length.

China has indicated that security is a primary interest in the region through its initiative in establishing the Shanghai Cooperation Organization (SCO) with Kazakhstan, Uzbekistan, Kyrgyzstan, Tajikistan, and Russia (pp. 6–7). Concerns regarding China's Muslim Uighur separatists, as well as concerns of U.S. encirclement, underpin China's efforts to promote regional security cooperation (pp. 4–6, 9–10). China has also moved aggressively to expand its economic interests in the region through commodity trade and agreements to import oil via pipeline from Kazakhstan (pp. 7–8).

Iran has a similar perspective toward its Central Asian neighbors. Stability in Afghanistan lies at the heart of Iran's concerns, as the Taliban has historically been anathema to Iran (p. 12). Iran maintains that an international, United Nations–led military presence should remain in Afghanistan to prevent a deterioration of the security situation (pp. 11–12). However, U.S. presence there and in Central Asia creates concern in Iran that U.S. intentions are to surround and isolate Iran rather than enhance regional security (p. 16). To increase its leverage in the region, Iran is developing economic links with each country in Central Asia. Transport links are another important initiative, with routes being developed via Afghanistan, connecting Iranian ports and landlocked Uzbekistan (pp. 13–16).

India shares Iran's concerns regarding the threat of militants based in Afghanistan. However, India welcomes U.S. presence in the region as a stabilizing influence (p. 34). Economic ties are growing, and India is developing transport and energy links to the region via Iran and Afghanistan (pp. 33–34). The Central Asian states have close relations with India dating to the years of the Soviet Union and the Afghan war, a history that negatively affects their relations with Pakistan.

Pakistan's relations with Central Asia suffer from lingering memories in the region of Pakistan's role in supporting the Taliban and Islamic militancy in general. Uzbekistan, Tajikistan, and Kyrgyzstan all remain suspicious of Pakistan's regional intentions, and trade with Pakistan has been weak as a result (p. 25). The establishment of the Karzai government in Kabul has been a blow to Pakistan's regional security strategy. Whereas the Taliban regime would have been friendly to Pakistan's interests, the current government is more open to ties with India (p. 23). Although Pakistan is moving to overcome its regional reputation, robust cooperation will take time and effort (p. 26).

Afghanistan remains critical to the future of Central Asia and its neighbors, as instability in Afghanistan has the potential to destabilize the region (pp. 19–20). A potent combination of drugs, weapons, and militants traverse Afghanistan and cross into Central Asia and beyond. Uzbekistan, Tajikistan, and Kyrgyzstan fear that Islamic militants trained in Afghanistan may slip back across their borders (p. 20). Iran remains apprehensive that hostile, anti-Shia elements may take control of Afghanistan, putting Iranian security at risk (p. 12).

And Pakistan and India both compete to ensure that the Afghan regime in power is friendly to their interests (pp. 26, 29). Although the countries across Asia do not agree on how to secure Afghanistan against threats, unanimous agreement exists on the fact that a stable Afghanistan is critical to their own security interests.

The U.S. presence has led both the Central Asian states and their neighbors to ponder how long the United States plans to keep troops in the region. U.S. intentions in the region have been interpreted in various ways. Both China and Iran are apprehensive that U.S. military presence and security interests in the area have the dual purpose of containment (pp. 3, 9–10, 11–12, 16). Conversely, Afghanistan would like to see a continued strong role for the United States in combating militancy and fostering stability (p. 22), and Pakistan and India see the potential for security cooperation with the United States in the region (pp. 27, 34). Despite the divergent perspectives of their Asian neighbors, the Central Asian states continue to see a role for the United States in promoting stability in the region.

Acknowledgments

No effort of this scope can be carried out without significant assistance. The RAND research team, which includes, in addition to the author of this monograph, Kamil Akramov, Sergej Mahnovski, Theodore Karasik, David Shlapak, and Prerna Singh, wants to thank, first of all, our project monitors at AF/XOX, particularly Col Anthony Hinen, Col Donald Jordan, Maj Gen Gould, Lt Col John Jerakis, and Lt Col Lon Stonebraker, who helped guide this research. We are also grateful to colleagues at the Office of the Secretary of Defense, the Joint Staff, the Defense Intelligence Agency, Central Command (CENTCOM), Central Command Air Forces (CENTAF), and European Command (EUCOM), who helped in expanding our knowledge and supported us at home and in the field. In addition, staff at the State Department, the Central Intelligence Agency, the Defense Intelligence Agency, the National Security Council, the U.S. Agency for International Development, the Department of Commerce, (including the Business Information Service for the Newly Independent States [BISNIS]), and the U.S. Treasury were generous with their time and their insights as were Ambassador Joseph Hulings, Robinder Bhatty, Daniel Burghardt, LTC Jon E. Chicky, and Scott Horton. Professor Philip Micklin, emeritus professor of geography at Western Michigan University, provided insights on water resources in Central Asia. Numerous conferences involving the Eurasia Group, DFI International, the Joint Staff, and the World Policy Institute Forum inform this research.

We are particularly grateful to the staff of the U.S. Embassies in Turkmenistan, Uzbekistan, and Kazakhstan, and most especially to the Defense Attache Offices in each of these countries, where we were very warmly welcomed. In Uzbekistan, we want to thank Ambassador John Herbst, LTC Robert W. Duggleby, Maj David Hinckley, Major Thomas J. Krajci, Ted Burkholter, John McKane, and Bill Lambert. We would like to thank the following individuals who assisted at Karshi-Khanabad, Uzbekistan: Lt. Col. Bill Berg, Lt. Col. Watts, and Maj. Greg Huston. In Turkmenistan, we are grateful to embassy staff including Ambassador Laura Kennedy and John Godfrey and most especially to MAJ Valen S. Tisdale. In Kazakhstan, our research would have been impossible without the help of COL Denise Donovan and Lt. Col Anthony Kwietniewski. We are also grateful to Ambassador Larry C. Napper and his staff, Angela Franklin Lord, Ken McNamara, and LTC William E. Lahue.

We are grateful to a number of representatives of Embassies in the United States and abroad. In Washington, D.C., staff at the Embassies of Turkey, Uzbekistan, Turkmenistan, and Kyrgyzstan deserve special thanks. In the region, we spoke to representatives at Embassies of the Russian Federation, Turkey, China, India, Pakistan, and Iran, and we are grateful to all of them for their time and insights. We also spoke to a broad range of officials, businesspeople, and specialists in the course of our travels and we want to extend our thanks to those, including Jean-Claude Beaujean, Matthew V. Brown, Saidrasul Bakiev, Ildar U. Baybekov, Deepak Chakraborti, Mila Eshonova, Dennis De Tray, Robert L. Horton, Talkgat Kaliev, Azizkhan Khankhodjaev, Merdan Khudaikuliev, Kiran Kaur, Lazat Kiinov, Nodirbek N. Ibragimov, Yelkin T. Malikov, Ruven Menikdiwela, Craig Murray, Colin Nelson, Donald Nicholson II, Robert S. Pace, Barbara Peitsch, David Pierce, Greg Rollheiser, Charles L. Rudd, Bakhram Salakhitdinov, Sanzhar Shalkarbekov, Nishanbay Sirajiddinov, Sean M. O'Sullivan, Bakhtiar Tukhtabaev, Olesya Tykhenko, William C. Veale, Michael Wilson, and Oksana Zenina.

Sarah Harting, Madeline Taylor, Miriam Schafer, and Terri Perkins made all of this flow smoothly with their capable administrative support. RAND library staff, including Roberta Shanman, Kristin McCool, Richard Bancroft, and Leroy Reyes, were essential in collecting data and information relevant for our analysis.

Abbreviations

BISNIS	Business Information Service for the Newly Independent States
CENTCOM	Central Command
CENTAF	Central Command Air Forces
CIA	Central Intelligence Agency
CNOOC	China National Offshore Oil Corporation
CNPC	China National Petroleum Corporation
ETIM	East Turkistan Islamic Movement
EUCOM	European Command
GAIL	Gas Authority of India Limited
IMU	Islamic Movement of Uzbekistan
IRP	Islamic Renaissance Party
ISAF	International Security Assistance Force
ISI	Inter-Services Intelligence
ITEC	Indian Technical and Economic Cooperation
K2	Karshi-Khanabad air base
NATO	North Atlantic Treaty Organization
NWFP	North West Frontier Province
ONGC	Oil and Natural Gas Commission
PAF	Project AIR FORCE
PRC	People's Republic of China
RATS	Regional Antiterrorist Structure
SCO	Shanghai Cooperation Organization
TDAPL	Turmenderman Ajanta Pharma Limited
UN	United Nations
WTO	World Trade Organization

CHAPTER ONE

Introduction

In order to understand the role that Central Asia plays in Asian security, it is critical to look at the region's relations with neighboring states such as China, Iran, India, Afghanistan, and Pakistan. To its neighbors, Central Asia presents economic opportunities and strategic challenges. Energy resources and prospective markets make the region attractive, although more from a long-term perspective than in an immediate sense. At the same time, concerns about the region's stability worry neighbors and others, who either are already affected or stand to be affected by the narcotics trade, weapons trade, organized crime, and other transnational threats that move through, and potentially issue from, the region. Finally, many states are concerned about the possible rise of Islamic radical groups in Central Asia, and these groups' potential to influence Muslim and ethnic Turkic populations in their own countries.

The U.S. presence and activity in the region has a significant impact here as well. Both the states of Central Asia and other interested parties view the development of Washington's relations with the region through the lens of their own competition, cooperation, and regional interests. From China's perspective, for example, close U.S. ties with the Central Asian states indicate an intention to encircle China. Thus, U.S. actions in Central Asia can affect U.S. relations with China, Iran, and others. This creates a complicated dynamic of interests and goals.

This monograph will consider interests in and ties with Central Asia on the part of China, Iran, Pakistan, Afghanistan, and India, and consider the effort to foster multinational cooperation in the region.

CHAPTER TWO

China

China's presence in Central Asia has visibly expanded in recent years, and it has become influential across the strategic, political, and economic landscape of the region.[1] China perceives itself as a player in an increased competition with the United States and Russia for influence in Central Asia, particularly as Operation Enduring Freedom and subsequent U.S.-led efforts to stabilize Afghanistan have provided a justification for an expanded U.S. presence in Asia. As the United States continues to closely engage the Afghanistan and Central Asian countries, China will remain apprehensive regarding U.S. interests and the possibility that the United States is attempting to surround China. Limiting the influence of the other great powers, and promoting security along its borders, will continue to be critical interests for the Chinese leadership. Rising security threats to China from terrorist groups add to the urgency for increased security cooperation with Kyrgyzstan, Kazakhstan, Tajikistan, and Uzbekistan. Continued instability in the region would also require a prolonged U.S. role and presence, a development that China would like to avoid. China's interests in Central Asia will be dominated by these security concerns in the coming years, while economic interests in the region will continue to be increasingly important.

---

[1] For an assessment of China's perspectives on Central Asia in the mid- to late-1990s, see Burles (1999).

China's Uighur Minority

China's primary concern regarding Central Asia is in ensuring the stability of the region, both to secure the country internally against insurgency and to ensure limited engagement in the region by the United States. China has historically had problems integrating politically and culturally its ethnic Muslim population in Xinjiang, and this domestic issue has affected China's relations with the neighboring states of Central Asia. The province, formally called the Xinjiang Uighur Autonomous Region, borders Kyrgyzstan, Kazakhstan, and Tajikistan. The Uighurs are a Turkic group that has resisted Chinese rule continuously since the first Chinese takeover of the region in 1759. Despite promises of self-determination made to ethnic minorities by the Chinese Communist Party during the Chinese civil war, Xinjiang and the other autonomous regions were forcibly integrated with China. In the 1950s, China began a program of mass migration of ethnic Han Chinese into Xinjiang, thereby increasing local resentment to Chinese rule. Although the Uighurs historically were the majority in the region, ethnic Chinese now comprise more than half of the population of Xinjiang and hold the majority of government and administrative positions.

With the defeat of the Soviet Union in Afghanistan, and the subsequent independence of the Central Asian states, the Uighur independence movement gained strength and inspiration. A separatist organization, the East Turkistan Islamic Movement (ETIM) formed and many militants began training alongside other Islamic militants in Afghanistan.[2] Uighur separatists have been charged with operating both in Xinjiang and across China's borders in Central Asia, launching attacks in Xinjiang and in neighboring countries. In 1990, a Uighur uprising in Xinjiang led to the death of more than 50 people in a confrontation with Chinese troops. Separatists are believed responsible for a series of bomb attacks in 1997 on Beijing, as well as other bombings and assassinations in Xinjiang.[3] The Chinese leader-

---

[2] George (1998).

[3] Gill and Oresman (2003, p. 16).

ship responded with harsh crackdowns on separatists and individuals involved in ethnic unrest, creating further violent reactions on the part of the Uighurs.

China's interest in suppressing the separatist movement in Xinjiang has affected relations with the Central Asian states, which all have Uighur minorities residing within their borders. Neighboring Kyrgyzstan has approximately 50,000 Uighurs, and China has pressured the Kyrgyz government to end any Kyrgyzstan-based support for Uighur separatism. The Kyrgyz government took action by cracking down on Uighur groups working in Kyrgyzstan, arresting Uighurs suspected of involvement in the East Turkistan movement.[4] Since September 11, 2001, violence from militant groups inside Kyrgyzstan has escalated, and countering Uighur groups has increasingly been in the interest of the Kyrgyz government. In June 2002, Uighur separatists allegedly killed a Chinese consul in Bishkek. In March 2003, a bus traveling in Kyrgyzstan was attacked, killing 21 Chinese aboard. Subsequent investigations indicated that the terrorists were ethnic Uighurs from China.[5] Other terrorist attacks in Bishkek and Osh have also been linked to Chinese separatists, although the evidence is unclear.[6] In November 2003, Kyrgyzstan increased efforts to counter Uighur and other separatist groups operating within its borders by banning several groups, including the Islamic Organization of Turkistan (formerly the Islamic Movement of Uzbekistan [IMU]), the Eastern Turkistan Islamic Party, and the Eastern Turkistan Liberation Organization.[7] After the revolution in Kyrgyzstan, China's concerns were heightened regarding its neighbor's ability to control separatist activity occurring within its territory. China is wary of the possibility that continued political instabil-

---

[4] Usaeva (2001).

[5] Kabar News Agency (2004).

[6] Interfax News Agency (2003).

[7] Ibraimov (2004).

ity in the region could be the basis for an increased U.S. military presence in the region.[8]

Furthermore, some Uighur separatist organizations, such as the Uighurstan Liberation Organization and the United Revolutionary Front of East Turkistan, are believed to have been operating from Kazakhstan.[9] Both Kyrgyzstan and Kazakhstan now maintain tighter border controls on the entry of Uighurs, whereas prior to September 11, 2001, people could cross these borders freely.

China will continue to focus on the ethnic issues connecting Xinjiang and Central Asia in the coming years. Xinjiang is central to China's strategic interests, as it includes China's nuclear testing ground in Lop Nor and is the base of many of the People's Republic of China's (PRC's) nuclear ballistic missiles. The province also holds critical importance for China's future energy needs, as Beijing is aiming to control considerable oil deposits that are believed to exist in Xinjiang. In addition, any oil pipelines to China from Kazakhstan will need to cross Xinjiang. Maintaining a stable and secure province will be vital to protecting these interests.

Regional Cooperation

China also has strong security and economic incentives for increasing its influence and leverage in Central Asia. Aside from its concerns regarding the linkages between extremist groups in Central Asia and China discussed above, the region presents ample opportunities for expanded exports, particularly because the Central Asian states are weak in the production of consumer goods. Establishing the regional Shanghai Cooperation Organization (SCO) was a major initiative taken by China to forward its security and economic interests in Central Asia. The organization is a loose association of Kazakhstan, Kyrgyzstan, Tajikistan, Uzbekistan, Russia, and China that seeks to

---

[8] "China Keeps Wary Eye on Kyrgyzstan Revolution" (2005).

[9] Karavan (2002).

provide a vehicle for expanded cooperation in security and economic affairs. The SCO established an organization called the Regional Antiterrorist Structure (RATS), headquartered in Tashkent, to facilitate cooperation among members and with other international institutions.[10] As part of these SCO initiatives, China embarked upon military counterterrorism exercises with Kazakhstan, Tajikistan, Kyrgyzstan, and Russia starting in August 2003.[11] This effort was a reaction to hijackings, kidnappings, and other violence by terrorist groups operating in Xinjiang and the Central Asian states. China has pursued joint military exercises with Kyrgyzstan in the past, in an effort to eliminate Islamic militants working in the border areas.[12] Although Uzbekistan declined to join the 2003 SCO counterterrorism exercises, China has expanded security cooperation with the country on a bilateral basis. Chinese authorities emphasize that the IMU and Uighur organizations are linked because they trained together in Afghanistan. China is increasingly interested in expanded cooperation among the United States, China, Russia, and Uzbekistan to intercept Uighur groups and individuals.

China is also turning to Central Asia as a source of its future energy and economic needs, although these interests remain subordinate to China's security interests in the region. Rapid economic growth has forced planners to look into diversified sources for energy imports, particularly from Kazakhstan. In recent years, China has received approximately half of its oil from the Middle East. To diversify its sources, Chinese state-owned major oil producers have entered a Kazakh-Chinese limited liability partnership for importing oil from Kazakhstan via the Atasu-Alashankou pipeline. In February 2005, KazTransOil announced that, in coordination with China Gas and Oil Exploration and Development Corporation, a pipeline for the transport of oil across Kazakhstan would be completed by December

---

[10] "China: Formation of Regional Antiterrorist Agency in Central Asia Completed" (2003).

[11] "China, Russia, Central Asian Nations Begin Antiterror Drills" (2003).

[12] Kozlova (2002).

2005, and oil could be transported to China by May 2006.[13] China National Petroleum Corporation (CNPC) is also in negotiations to supply China with gas from Kazakhstan. The rapid expansion of energy ties between the two countries has led to warming overall bilateral relations between China and Kazakhstan. China has made moves to develop energy ties with other nations in the region as well. China has initiated oil and gas projects in Turkmenistan, and the state of Xinjiang signed an agreement in November 2004 with Kyrgyzstan for the purchase of hydroelectric power in order to meet its own energy needs.[14]

In addition, China is creating economic partnerships with the republics and the region has grown as a market for Chinese consumer goods. Economic relations with the republics are a major focus for China and it is moving rapidly to create avenues for the expansion of exports from China into the region. Both China and Kyrgyzstan are members of the World Trade Organization (WTO), enabling bilateral trade. In recent years, China had developed a solid export trade in food and construction materials to Kyrgyzstan.[15] However, political instability after the revolution in Kyrgyzstan paralyzed border trade as traders waited for the restoration of order.[16] Trade between China and Kazakhstan has grown rapidly in recent years, and it is expected to rise further as Kazakhstan prepares to enter the WTO. For Uzbekistan, trade cooperation with China has become a priority. In June 2004, a Chinese delegation visited Uzbekistan to expand economic cooperation.[17] The Chinese delegation identified cooperation in oil and gas and credit and soft loans from China to Uzbekistan, education, and culture as priorities. Trade between Uzbekistan and China reached $575 million for 2004, and it has been increasing.[18]

---

[13] Kazakhstanskaya Pravda (2005).

[14] Kyrgyz Television First Channel (2004b).

[15] Interfax News Agency (2005).

[16] "Chinese Traders Await Long-Term Stability in Kyrgyzstan" (2005).

[17] Uzbek Television Second Channel (2004).

[18] "China's Trade with Uzbekistan in January 2005" (2005).

China provided approximately $600,000 in aid to Uzbekistan to assist in implementation of the projects.[19] In Tajikistan, a Chinese telecommunications company, the ZTE Corporation, has in recent years reconstructed all of the telephone exchanges in Dushanbe to assist in the modernization of Tajik communications networks.[20]

However, the rapid increase in the amount of Chinese consumer goods coming into Central Asia has also created concerns. The weak economies and manufacturing sectors in the Central Asian republics are poorly equipped to compete with the flood of low-cost Chinese goods that cross their borders. The countries of Central Asia are anxious that China is crushing their feeble industries and inhibiting the growth of new businesses. As insecurities with regard to China's economic strength grow, the countries are implementing trade restrictions to limit the flow of Chinese goods into their countries, although they often find that Chinese goods are entering their countries illegally as well as legally. Apprehension regarding China's economic prowess will remain a key issue in Central Asia's relations with China.

The U.S. Role

China remains suspicious of U.S. intentions in Central Asia and it is interested in limiting U.S. influence, insofar as possible (while extending its own contacts). Concerns are growing that the United States and the North Atlantic Treaty Organization (NATO) may be shifting focus from Europe to Central Asia. Although Uzbekistan formally evicted the United States from the air base at Karshi-Khanabad (K2) in July 2005, the situation continues to unfold.[21] In any case, the United States continues to have a military presence in Central Asia, a situation that China will be monitoring. Chinese concerns were heightened by the increasing role for NATO in Afghan

---

[19] "China Grants No-Strings Aid to Uzbekistan" (2003).

[20] Asia-Plus News Agency (2003a).

[21] Wright and Tyson (2005).

peacekeeping. Chinese officials state that the U.S. presence in Central Asia should be short-term, as not only China, but also Iran and Russia, are uncomfortable with an extended U.S. presence in the region after the Iraq war. They argue that the U.S. presence in Central Asia should be "a question of time, not level."[22] Because the focus for the region is on economic development, investment is needed most. In this context, Chinese officials believe that the U.S. military presence is not useful.

---

[22] Author interviews with Chinese officials and specialists in Central Asia, May 2003.

CHAPTER THREE

Iran

Iran has close historic and economic ties to Central Asia that provide a strong foundation for expanded relations. Persian empires reached across Central Asia, leaving a cultural and linguistic legacy that remains strongest in Tajikistan, and in the cities of Samarkand and Bukhara in Uzbekistan. Iranian diplomats continue to emphasize the cultural similarities that exist between the region and Iran as a reason for closer economic relations.[1] However, Iran's stand in highlighting its role in Central Asia's cultural heritage creates tension with Central Asian republics, who are apprehensive of an overbearing neighbor and interested in establishing themselves as independent states both politically and culturally.

An important strategic rationale also exists for Iran to improve diplomatic relations with the region. In the aftermath of the September 11 attacks, the United States increased its military presence in the region dramatically. With bases in Afghanistan and Kyrgyzstan, and significant numbers of U.S. troops in Iraq, Iran has found itself diplomatically isolated and virtually surrounded by U.S. armed forces. Hostile relations between the United States and Iran create an incentive for Tehran to foster close ties with its neighbors in Central Asia in order to ensure its security and economic interests.[2] Because stability in Afghanistan is critical for the security of the region, Iran's leadership has emphasized that a continued international presence in

---

[1] Author interviews with Iranian officials and specialists in Central Asia, May 2003.

[2] IRNA (2005a).

Afghanistan is necessary, albeit under United Nations (UN) supervision. The countries of Central Asia view Iran as a central actor in Afghanistan and key to economic growth and trade in the region, but have deep concerns regarding Iran's developing nuclear capacity and regional ambitions.[3]

Stability in Afghanistan is a key interest for Iran, and it informs Iran's policy toward Central Asia. During the early 1990s, Iran and the Central Asian states shared a common interest in resisting Pashtun fundamentalist domination of Afghanistan. The fundamentalist Sunni Pashtuns were known for their persecution of the Shia minorities of Afghanistan, leading Iran to lend its support to the Shia Hazara faction and the Persian-speaking Tajiks.[4] After the takeover of Kabul by the Taliban, the regional security situation quickly deteriorated. The 1998 murder of nine Iranian diplomats by the Taliban created a furor in Iran, bringing Iran and Afghanistan close to war. Anger at the militant group led Iran to place 270,000 troops on the border with Afghanistan in a threat to invade.[5] Although tensions did not escalate into conflict, relations between the Taliban and Iran remain extremely hostile.[6] In an effort to undermine the Taliban, Iran sent weapons through Tajikistan to the Northern Alliance forces in Afghanistan beginning in the mid-1990s. Iran, Tajikistan, India, and Russia shared a similar goal of supporting Ahmad Shah Massoud during that time, and they played complementary roles in combating the Taliban.[7] However, Pakistan also became the focus of Iranian ire: The Inter-Services Intelligence (ISI) was well known to have been

---

[3] Author interviews with Central Asian officials and specialists in Central Asia, summer 2003.

[4] Rashid (2000, p. 200).

[5] "Iran to Keep Troops on Afghanistan Border Until Security Ensured" (1998).

[6] Author interviews with Iranian scholars, fall 2003.

[7] "Iran Supplying Arms to Anti-Taleban Forces Through Tajikistan" (1999).

supporting the Taliban, and Pakistani militants had been involved in the murder of the Iranian diplomats in 1998.[8]

Iran continued to play a role in Afghan politics under the government of President Hamid Karzai. In recent years, the warlord Ismail Khan, a previous governor of Herat with close ties to Iran, smuggled thousands of weapons into Afghanistan from Iran in order to tip the power balance in his favor.[9] However, in December 2004, Ismail Khan was appointed a member of the Afghan Cabinet, a move that was meant to bring his allegiances closer to those of the central government and decrease his overall influence.[10]

Regional Cooperation

Diplomatic and economic isolation from the United States has forced Iran to expand its business and security links with other states in order to remain economically viable. Iranian businesses have been successful in the commodity and energy trades in particular, competing for influence in the region with Russia and Turkey. Trade ties have grown rapidly between Iran and the Central Asian states in the past decade, strengthening and broadening diplomatic relations. However, tensions between Iran and various countries in the region remain. In particular, the division of the Caspian Sea boundaries is a major source of disagreement between Iran, Turkmenistan, Kazakhstan, Azerbaijan, and Russia. Iran insists that the demarcations are the same as those agreed upon by the Soviet Union and Iran in 1921 and 1941.

Uzbekistan considers Iran to be a critical access route to world markets and fosters a close relationship with that country. Trade between Iran and Uzbekistan is strong, with the total for 2004 reaching

---

[8] Rashid (2000, p. 74).

[9] Shah (2004).

[10] "President Karzai Announces New Afghan Cabinet" (2004).

$300 million.[11] Both countries have a strong interest in cooperating to build transportation infrastructure, with plans to build a north-south road from Iran through Afghanistan to Uzbekistan. Iran has invested in the construction of the route connecting Tashkent with Mazar-e-Sharif and Herat in Afghanistan, traversing the Iranian port of Chabahar and ending at Bandar Abbas in Iran. The transportation network will include rail links and will provide much needed access for Uzbek goods to the Iranian ports of Bandar Abbas and Chabahar.[12] Uzbekistan and Iran also share security interests in countering regional terrorist activities and drug smuggling, creating the basis for bilateral security cooperation in these areas.[13]

Trade and transport have become an increasingly important component of relations with Tajikistan. Tajikistan and Iran share close cultural ties and both countries speak the same language, creating a strong basis for commerce and investment. Strategic relations were expanded during the war against the Taliban: Both Tehran and Dushanbe were united in supporting anti-Taliban factions. These ethnic and linguistic bonds have proven useful in expanding relations in the economic arena as well.

Trade between the two countries was approximately $100 million in 2004, and initiatives in transportation links between the two countries are likely to lead to greater exchange in the coming years.[14] Iran in 2003 agreed to give Tajikistan $31 million for development of transport, and in 2005 it agreed to another $5 million in transport grants.[15] In January 2005, Iran, Russia, and Tajikistan agreed to build a hydroelectric power station in Tajikistan in two stages. Russia will

---

[11] "Uzbek, Iranian Businesses, Officials Meet in Uzbekistan" (2005)

[12] Author interviews with officials and specialists in Central Asia; Vision of the Islamic Republic of Iran Network 1 (2004).

[13] IRNA (2005b).

[14] IRNA (2005c).

[15] Asia-Plus News Agency (2003b); Tajik Television (2004).

build Sangtuda 1 followed by Iranian construction of Sangtuda 2.[16] Iran is also involved in the construction of the Anzob tunnel, which would connect Iran to Kazakhstan and Kyrgyzstan, and Tajikistan to South Asian ports through Afghanistan and Pakistan, providing greater trade access throughout the region.[17] The new tunnel is currently under construction by the Iranian company Sabir International. When completed, it is estimated to cut travel time between Iran and Central Asia by four to five hours. The assistance package, of which $10 million is aid and the remaining $21 million is a loan, would also be used for the construction of other Tajik roads.[18]

Bilateral relations with Turkmenistan have deepened with recent agreements on trade in electricity, cooperation against drug trafficking, and the building of a "friendship dam" on the Iran-Turkmenistan border. The two countries agreed to electricity cooperation in 2003 and inaugurated the supply of 562 meters per kilowatt hour (m/kWh) per year via the Balkanabat-Gonbad power transmission line. In 2004, a second power transmission line was built to provide electricity from Turkmenistan to Iran, with an expected annual export of 375m/kWh.[19] The Dousti (friendship) dam was built with costs shared equally by Iran and Turkmenistan, and was officially inaugurated in April 2005.[20]

Kazakhstan and Iran have fostered deepening relations in the past few years. Disagreements on the Caspian Sea issue remain to be resolved, yet both countries maintain positive security, energy, and trade relationships, and both countries have discussed cooperation in combating terrorism, drug trafficking, and organized crime.[21] Iran and Kazakhstan have an energy swap wherein Kazakhstan supplies oil

---

[16] Tajik Television (2005).

[17] "Tajikistan: Iran Allocates Total of $30 Million for Tunnel" (2003); Avesta (2004).

[18] Asia-Plus News Agency (2003b).

[19] Turkmen Government (2004).

[20] Vision of the Islamic Republic of Iran Network 1 (2004); "Iran, Turkmenistan Inaugurate 'Dam of Friendship' on Border" (2005).

[21] IRNA (2004b).

to Iran via the Caspian Sea to the port of Neka, and in return, Kazakhstan receives the equivalent amount of oil via the port of Kharq, Iran, in the Persian Gulf.[22] Overall bilateral trade stands at $780 million, with more than 100 Iranian companies active in Kazakhstan.[23]

Relations with Kyrgyzstan have been warm in recent years, although currently Iran is closely observing developments in Kyrgyzstan following the overthrow of the Akayev regime. In 2004, Iran gave $1 million in aid to Kyrgyzstan for the development of that country.[24] Discussions remain underway for Iran's energy trade with Kyrgyzstan, with the two main options being the Uzbekistan-Turkmenistan route or a Tajikistan-Afghanistan route.[25]

The U.S. Role

U.S. involvement in Central Asia complicates Iran's dealings with other countries in the region, leading some to note with concern that close ties with Iran might alienate the United States, even as they recognize the need for peaceful and positive relations with this neighbor. The Central Asian states are apprehensive that tensions between the United States and Iran could eventually escalate, thereby destabilizing the entire region. The evolving situation in Afghanistan also remains a vital interest for Iran, and it has expressed concern that the conflict in Iraq will draw international attention and resources away from stabilizing and securing Afghanistan. However, Iranian officials oppose a sustained U.S. military presence in the region, particularly U.S. bases in Central Asia and Afghanistan. Iranian officials are apprehensive that the United States intends to maintain hegemony and inhibit Ira-

---

[22] "Kazakhstan to Build Two Oil Terminals in Iran" (2004).

[23] "Kazakhstan Keen to Boost Trade Ties with Iran" (2005).

[24] Kyrgyz Television First Channel (2004).

[25] IRNA (2004a).

nian interests in the region.[26] Nonetheless, there is no evidence that Iran is making efforts to counter U.S. activities in Central Asia.

---

[26] Author interviews with Iranian officials in Central Asia, summer 2003.

CHAPTER FOUR
Afghanistan

The relationship between the Central Asian states and their neighbors is complex and heavily influenced by the situation in Afghanistan. Afghanistan forms the link between regions, and it has endured a great deal of meddling from various sides, as in the past few decades, the United States, Pakistan, India, Iran, Russia, Uzbekistan, and other countries have attempted to push for a friendly government in Afghanistan. Since September 11, 2001, and the fall of the Taliban, Afghanistan has also gained in importance as a feasible key transport route for increased trade and security cooperation between the countries of Central Asia and India and Pakistan.[1]

Stability in Afghanistan has had a profound effect on Central Asian security as both religious radicalism and drugs emanating from Afghanistan threaten the region. During the Afghan-Soviet war, the United States in effect, through Pakistan, supported fundamentalist Islamic teachings and military training of Afghan, Pakistani, and other Central Asian militants in an effort to expel the Soviet Union from Afghanistan.[2] The growth of Islamic fundamentalism from the Afghan-Soviet war accelerated the spread of a religious ideology throughout the formerly communist countries. The Taliban trained Uzbek, Tajik, and Uighur radicals, spurring the growth of destabi-

---

[1] Author interviews with officials and specialists in Central Asia, summer 2003.

[2] Author interviews with former senior U.S. officials; Hyman (2001); Rashid (2002).

lizing fundamentalist movements throughout the region.[3] In 1992, leaders of the Islamic Renaissance Party (IRP) fled Tajikistan to take refuge and regroup in Afghanistan, Pakistan, Iran, and Russia.[4] During the 1990s, Afghanistan also became a haven for the IMU.[5]

Uzbekistan, Kazakhstan, Kyrgyzstan, and Tajikistan all moved to support the anti-Taliban Northern Alliance in the 1990s in the hopes of defeating the fundamentalist threat.[6] The Central Asian states remain concerned by the continued presence of militants in Afghanistan and, now, Pakistan, and also by the booming drug trade that passes through Afghanistan and Central Asia into Europe and Russia.[7] Narcotics flow from Afghanistan via multiple routes in the region to foreign markets, and populations of these transit corridors are increasingly consumers of the drugs as well. Traffickers transport opiates north through Tajikistan and Kyrgyzstan on to Russia, and west through Iran and Turkmenistan to Turkey and Europe.[8] Tajikistan has made efforts to stem the flow of drugs across its border from Afghanistan, establishing two antidrug agencies in Afghanistan to coordinate military and nonmilitary operations with international troops and Afghan forces in the border areas.[9]

Since the fall of the Taliban, many local leaders have retained considerable power and maintain some ability to destabilize the Kabul government. In addition, various renegade militant groups and remnants of the Taliban continue to operate in parts of Afghanistan, particularly near the Pakistani border. The ability of these groups to move nimbly across the border to evade counterterrorism forces and border patrols has been a cause for consternation among Afghani-

---

[3] Rashid (2002, p. 174).

[4] Rashid (2002, p. 174).

[5] Rashid (2002, p. 174).

[6] Author interviews with officials and specialists in Central Asia, summer 2003.

[7] ITAR-TASS News Agency (2002).

[8] Kyrgyz Television (2005).

[9] Voice of the Islamic Republic of Iran (2005).

stan's neighbors.[10] Uzbekistan, Tajikistan, Kazakhstan, and Kyrgyz-stan are concerned that Afghanistan could revert to a haven for ter-rorist training, sending the militants back into their countries to de-stabilize regimes.[11]

A political vacuum in Afghanistan has traditionally drawn its neighboring countries in to compete for influence. Uzbekistan, Kyrgyzstan, and Tajikistan have an interest in fostering trade and transport linkages both with and through Afghanistan, but they face difficulties in maintaining security for the routes.[12] Iran has been suc-cessful in moving forward with an agreement to trade goods with Uz-bekistan through Afghanistan. This agreement has facilitated Uzbeki-stan's access to needed ports for export.[13]

There is considerable interest in Afghanistan's role as a transit country for energy trade from Central Asia to South Asia. The main proposal puts forth the construction of a trans-Afghan pipeline to supply gas from Turkmenistan to Pakistan via Afghanistan.[14] The plan is very attractive because South Asia is forecast to be a major consumer of Central Asian and Iranian energy, and Afghanistan needs to diversify its sources of income away from the drug trade. However, roads and infrastructure in Afghanistan must be rebuilt and secured before transport can begin.[15] In addition, Pakistan and India now compete for influence in Afghanistan, causing consternation within the Afghan government. Pashtuns in Afghanistan draw sup-port from Pakistan, including training and financial assistance, whereas the government of Hamid Karzai has benefited from India's initiatives in the medical and other arenas.

---

[10] Vecherniy Bishkek (2002).

[11] Author interviews with officials in Uzbekistan, December 2004; author interviews with officials and specialists in Central Asia, summer 2003.

[12] Author interviews with officials and specialists in Central Asia, summer 2003.

[13] Uzbek Television (2005).

[14] "Talks Held on Turkmenistan-Afghanistan-Pakistan Gas Pipeline" (2005).

[15] Author interview with development bank official in Central Asia, May 2003.

The U.S. Role

The U.S. interest in preventing a return of militant training camps and groups such as the Taliban and al Qaeda indicates that a continued U.S. military presence in Afghanistan is necessary in the near term to help maintain stability. The government of Hamid Karzai has repeatedly requested a larger U.S. and international presence to assist in maintaining security and in the rebuilding of Afghanistan. As stability of the central government in Kabul is critical to the security of its neighbors, Uzbekistan, Kazakhstan, Tajikistan, and Kyrgyzstan have also emphasized that a continued international presence in Afghanistan would be beneficial, and an early withdrawal disastrous.[16] While problems persist in the region despite U.S. presence and assistance, the countries of Central Asia have noted that they would be even less capable of preventing the growth of illegal trade and extremist groups throughout the region in the absence of a U.S. role in Afghanistan.[17] Thus, it is likely that these states, the United States, and other countries such as Russia and Iran, who share an interest in promoting peace and security in Afghanistan, will have reasons and arenas in which to cooperate.

---

[16] Author interviews with Central Asian officials, summer 2003; Tajik Television First Channel (2002); "Different Views on Anti-Terrorist Operation in Afghanistan at Kazakh Round Table" (2002).

[17] Author interviews with Uzbek officials, December 2004; author interviews with Central Asian officials, spring–summer 2003.

CHAPTER FIVE

Pakistan

Pakistan's relations with the Central Asian states have been complicated by its historic role in Afghanistan and in supporting Islamist groups. The military in Pakistan long considered Afghanistan to be a critical region for ensuring Pakistan's security, as it could provide "strategic depth" against its rival India. In case of a major military engagement with India, friendly relations with Afghanistan would provide the Pakistani military with the ability to fall back and regroup.[1] Until the rise of the Taliban, however, Afghanistan remained a close friend of India. Instead of providing strategic depth, Pakistan viewed Afghanistan as part of a larger Indian strategy to encircle Pakistan. Unable to alter the diplomatic situation with Kabul, Pakistan worked closely with militant groups through the 1980s and 1990s to undermine the Afghan government and replace it with a pro-Pakistan regime.[2]

Pakistan's support of militancy and religious fundamentalism in Central Asia began in the 1980s, when funding from the Central Intelligence Agency (CIA) was funneled through ISI, the Pakistani intelligence organization, to help train mujahideen in Afghanistan as combatants against the Soviet Union.[3] Militants from Uzbekistan, Kyrgyzstan, Tajikistan, China, and various other countries began

---

[1] Author interviews with Indian and Pakistani officials, summer 2003.

[2] Rashid (2001).

[3] Kaplan (2000); Rashid (2001).

training alongside Pakistanis and Afghans in Afghan military training camps.[4] In the 1990s, Uzbekistan's efforts to combat the IMU were complicated by ISI support for the group. Uzbek Islamic activists and Tahir Yuldeshev, a prominent leader, moved to Pakistan with support from the ISI from 1995 to 1998.[5] In the following years, the IMU was able to operate and strengthen its forces inside Afghanistan. After the U.S. campaign in Afghanistan, several hundred members of the IMU fled from Afghanistan to Pakistan in order to avoid interception by U.S. troops.[6] In addition, IMU leader Yuldeshev is reported to have moved his operations to Pakistan.[7] The inability of Pakistani authorities to control militant Islamic groups operating in Pakistani territory has been an issue of intense concern for Uzbekistan and Tajikistan, as well as other countries in the region.[8] In 2004, Pakistan captured a number of Uzbek militants in South Waziristan and Multan, and other Uzbek militants are expected to be residing in various parts of Pakistan.[9] Continued training of Uzbek and Tajik fundamentalist militants in the ungoverned areas of Pakistan's North West Frontier Province (NWFP) will continue to pose a destabilizing force for the new Afghan government as well.[10] However, the Pakistani and Uzbek governments have strengthened cooperation against terrorism in talks between Presidents Musharraf and Karimov in March 2005.[11] The Uzbek government is increasingly moving toward a closer rela-

---

[4] Rohde (2002); Rashid (2002, p. 174).

[5] Rashid (2002, p. 140).

[6] Kozlova (2003).

[7] Author interviews with Uzbek officials, March 2005; Baker (2003).

[8] Author interviews with Central Asian officials, December 2004 and summer 2003.

[9] "Uzbekistan Seeks Information about Militants Arrested in Pakistan" (2004); Associated Press of Pakistan (2004).

[10] Anis (2003); "Armitage Visits President Musharraf at Army Headquarters: Pakistani Official" (2003).

[11] "Pakistan and Uzbekistan Vow to Intensify Efforts Against Terrorism" (2005).

tionship with Pakistan in order to improve Pakistan's ability to assist in counterterror efforts.[12]

These troubles have been exacerbated by an encumbered investment climate in the region as well as by regional apprehension toward Pakistan. Security concerns regarding Pakistan's role in fomenting fundamentalism in the region have hampered Pakistan's ability to build close financial relations with Tajikistan and Uzbekistan in particular.[13] And although Pakistan's leaders are now embarking upon initiatives to expand trade, transport, and energy linkages with the countries of the region, progress remains slow and hampered by broader regional security concerns. Until stability is established in Afghanistan, transport through Pakistan will face great obstacles.

Domestic economic barriers to entry in the countries of Central Asia will also need to be addressed before significant trade and investment is possible. In the early 1990s, many Pakistani firms and the Bank of Pakistan moved into the region expecting rapid liberalization and acceptance of their services. After attempting to conduct business in Turkmenistan and Uzbekistan for several years, many firms resorted to looking for an exit strategy.[14] This perspective may be shifting, however. Pakistani President Musharraf indicated an interest in fostering bilateral trade during his March 2005 visit to Uzbekistan, and Uzbek officials have stated a similar interest.[15] Pakistan has also been making overtures to Tajikistan, holding a "Made in Pakistan" exhibition there in April 2005, and has signed a memorandum of understanding for the Tajik sale of electricity to Pakistan.[16] Economic relations with Kazakhstan had also been improving, but this may be affected by the January 2005 unsolved murder of a Kazakh diplomat

---

[12] Author interviews with Uzbek officials, March 2005.

[13] Author interviews with Central Asian officials, spring and summer 2003.

[14] Author interviews with Pakistani officials.

[15] PTV World (2005).

[16] "'Made in Pakistan' Exhibition Begins in Tajikistan" (2005); "Pakistan signs MOU With Tajikistan to Buy Power" (2005).

in Islamabad.[17] Pakistan's efforts to expand ties with Kyrgyzstan include a planned road linking Kyrgyzstan to the Pakistani ports of Karachi and Gwadar, and possible supply of electricity to Pakistan.[18]

This new turn in relations may indicate a Pakistani interest in fostering warmer relations in Central Asia to avoid being isolated in the region. Pakistan's role in training militants and supporting the Taliban created strained relations with the Central Asian states. These new diplomatic initiatives could help Pakistan rebuild ties as a first step toward becoming more competitive with India, Afghanistan, Iran, and China for trade and influence in the region.

Energy serves as another critical link between Pakistan and the countries of Central Asia. Pakistan has an interest in the building of a gas pipeline from Turkmenistan through Afghanistan to Pakistan and India. This plan has generated much interest and debate, although the feasibility of the plan is still under discussion by investors. A serious issue under consideration is that the long-term tensions between India and Pakistan make the deal risky for India. In addition, instability and lawlessness in Afghanistan mean that securing the pipeline would be extremely difficult. These factors play a critical role in India's decision to invest in the venture, which affects the profitability of the venture. The amelioration of relations between Pakistan and India in 2004 and 2005 has increased the feasibility of gas pipelines traversing Pakistan en route to India. Whereas India was a reluctant consumer in past years due to their apprehension that Pakistan could sabotage their energy supply, the Indian government now appears more willing to consider an energy agreement with Pakistan as a transit route. In the interim, Pakistan, Afghanistan, and Turkmenistan have moved forward in discussing the agreement.[19]

---

[17] Interfax-Kazakhstan News Agency (2005a).

[18] "Pakistan-Kyrgyzstan Sign Agreements, Vow to Expand Bilateral Trade" (2005).

[19] PTV (2005).

The U.S. Role

A continued U.S. presence in Central Asia presents domestic complications for Pakistan. U.S. forces active on the Afghan-Pakistan border have been forced, on occasion, to enter Pakistan to pursue militants, causing uproar in Pakistan over national sovereignty.[20] The government of Pakistan is under domestic pressure to limit its cooperation with the United States in pursuing Taliban and other militants in the area, and there is considerable support from the leaders and public in the Pakistan's NWFP and Baluchistan for the Taliban.[21] Insofar as Pakistan is successful in reigning in extremist groups and activities in Pakistan and Afghanistan, relations between Pakistan and the countries of Central Asia may see improvement. If, however, the situation in Pakistan worsens, Central Asian states will view Pakistan as an increasing threat.

---

[20] "Pakistan Protests U.S. Troops Firing in South Waziristan" (2005); "Pakistan Finds 'Unacceptable' U.S. Military Incursions" (2004).

[21] Gall (2003); "Pamphlets Urging Attacks on U.S. Troops Handed Out in Pakistani Mosques" (2003).

CHAPTER SIX

India

India, too, sees Central Asia through the lenses of economics and security. Like other neighbors, it has sought to expand counterterrorism cooperation and improve access to energy resources. India views Central Asia in the broader context of the militancy in Afghanistan and support for fundamentalism in Pakistan. Pakistan has historically suspected India of attempting to surround Pakistan by developing close ties with the countries of Central Asia and Afghanistan, though the Indian government denies harboring this intention.[1] According to Indian analysts, broader economic and political interests provide the foundation for closer Indian ties with the region.[2]

India's relations with the countries of the region are positive, and relatively uncomplicated, as there are no major issues of dispute between India and the Central Asian republics. Historically, India's relations with the countries of Central Asia were also close. Prior to 1990, India's warm relationship with the Soviet Union laid the foundation for amicable ties, and Pakistan's support for Islamic fundamentalist movements in the region served to push the countries closer to India.[3] The current security imperatives facing India are common with those of the Central Asian states, as well as Russia, China, and Iran, implying that greater security and economic cooperation is

---

[1] Author interviews with Indian officials, 2003–2004.

[2] Author interviews with Indian officials and specialists, 2003–2004.

[3] Author interviews with officials in Central Asia, 2003–2004.

probable. India has indicated an interest in joining the SCO regional grouping, where it currently maintains an observer status, and Uzbekistan, Kyrgyzstan, Tajikistan, and Kazakhstan have indicated their support for India joining the organization.[4] Kazakhstan and Tajikistan have also stated their support for India's bid for a seat on the UN Security Council.[5]

Regional Cooperation

Counterterrorism cooperation has been the main security concern for India with regard to Central Asia, and cooperative security initiatives have already begun with Tajikistan, Uzbekistan, Kyrgyzstan, and Kazakhstan. India's security is closely tied to the instability in the region between Afghanistan and Pakistan. Close cooperation between the Taliban and Pakistan before September 11, 2001, contributed to terrorist attacks against India during that time.[6] Many Pakistani militants received training in Afghan and Pakistani training camps prior to joining the militancy in Jammu and Kashmir.[7] In 1999, terrorists hijacked Indian Airlines flight IC-814, departing from Kathmandu, landing the plane in Kandahar in Afghanistan.[8] The hostages aboard the plane were later exchanged for three terrorists held by India.[9] The incident highlighted for Indian planners the importance of fostering close ties with Afghanistan, and the necessity of denying the Central Asian region to terrorist groups. Various Pakistan-supported terrorist groups active in Kashmir, such as Lashkar-e-Taiba and Jaish-e-

---

[4] "India, Uzbekistan Vow to Fight Terrorism, Sign 12 Accords" (2005); "Tajikistan Welcomes India Joining Shanghai's Club" (2003); Kyrgyz AKI Press (2003).

[5] "Tajikistan, Kazakhstan Endorse India's Bid for Seat in UNSC" (2005).

[6] Meyer (2000).

[7] Haniffa (2000).

[8] "Pak Police Identifies IA Hijacker as Suspect in Pearl Case" (2002).

[9] Bedi (2002).

Mohammed, received military training in Afghan camps alongside Central Asian militant groups such as the IMU, as well as Tajik and Uighur militants.[10]

India and Tajikistan have historically cooperated against the Taliban in Afghanistan, and have continued security cooperation against their remnants. During the Afghan war against the Soviets, both countries maintained a key interest in supporting the Northern Alliance and Tajik tribes against the Pashtun Taliban, an interest shared with Iran. India supplied approximately $8 million for high-altitude warfare equipment to the Northern Alliance through Tajikistan, and provided as other assistance to combat the Taliban forces.[11] Since then, India has embarked upon extensive military cooperation with Tajikistan, reportedly establishing its first military facility there in 2002. The base is believed to be in Farkhor, along the northern border with Afghanistan.[12] However, the government of Tajikistan has denied that India has a military facility there and has stated that India has simply assisted the country with rebuilding a military airfield at Ayni, near Dushanbe.[13] India for years had kept a secret military hospital in Farkhor for the treatment of Northern Alliance soldiers injured in the Afghan war, which has now moved to Kabul.[14] The base had been used for sending relief assistance to Afghanistan, but likely also represented India's longer-term security interests in preventing a resurgence of Taliban rule or preventing another hostile group from taking power in Kabul. In 2002, India agreed to train Tajik defense personnel, service their Russian military equipment, and provide English instruction to the military. Under this 2002 agreement, Tajikistan sent 50 cadets to India in 2003 for military

---

[10] Rohde (2002); "Delhi Tracks Al Qaeda, Jaish Links," (2001).

[11] Bedi (2002).

[12] "Great Gamer India Sets Up First Overseas Base" (2002).

[13] "India, Tajikistan to Intensify Defence Cooperation" (2003).

[14] Bedi (2002); Rahman (2002).

training as engineers, paratroopers, and signalmen.[15] In 2003, India conducted joint military exercises with Tajikistan.

Agreements with Uzbekistan for joint training, exchanges of experts, joint exercises, development and production of equipment, and information sharing were also aimed at countering terrorist activities.[16] Both countries have a common interest in curbing support for Islamic militants from within Pakistan and Afghanistan. Uzbekistan has claimed that Pakistanis have been involved in the training of IMU militants, while India is concerned with terrorism in Jammu and Kashmir supported by Pakistan.[17] Agreements to increase defense cooperation between the two countries led to the sale of six Uzbek-made IL-78 air-to-air refueling aircraft in 2003 for use by the Indian Air Force.[18]

Economically, India has a growing presence in Central Asia in the energy and pharmaceutical sectors. Trade in consumer goods is increasing but constrained by economic barriers, particularly in Turkmenistan and Uzbekistan. Trade with Uzbekistan amounted to more than $121 million in 2004, with more than 30 Uzbek-Indian joint ventures in Uzbekistan. A significant source of revenue for India is in pharmaceutical sales from Ajanta Pharma and Reddy Labs.[19] The two countries are considering Indian gas exploration in Uzbekistan through India's public sector Oil and Natural Gas Commission (ONGC) and Gas Authority of India Limited (GAIL).

ONGC has moved forward to stake claims in four of Kazakhstan's oil fields as well.[20] Both countries are developing bilateral trade

---

[15] "Tajik-India" (2003); Asia-Plus News Agency (2003c).

[16] "India, Uzbekistan Sign Pacts on Defense, Trade" (2005).

[17] Author interviews with officials and specialists in Uzbekistan, December 2004.

[18] Uzbek Radio (2003).

[19] "Uzbekistan President Starts State Visit to India" (2005).

[20] "Now, India Makes a Beeline for Kazakh Oil" (2005).

in mechanical engineering and pharmaceuticals, and in the defense sectors; total bilateral trade in 2003 stood at $79 million.[21]

Bilateral trade between India and Turkmenistan for 2003 totaled $19.1 million.[22] The joint venture between the Indian company Ajanta Pharma and the Ministry of Health in Turkmenistan, named Turkmenderman Ajanta Pharma Limited (TDAPL), currently provide approximately half of the pharmaceutical needs of Turkmenistan.[23] However, difficulty in converting currency has limited the joint venture's ability to procure raw materials and expand production. India has widened information exchange programs with Turkmenistan, establishing the $0.5 million Turkmen–Indian Industrial Training Centre as a gift to train Turkmen in basic skills, in the manufacturing of tools and components, and in business practices for small and medium enterprises, and provide financial, computer, and language training through its Indian Technical and Economic Cooperation (ITEC) program.[24]

Development of a gas pipeline connecting India to Turkmenistan has been an issue of intense focus, though the viability of such a plan is yet unclear. India remains concerned that such a pipeline would need to traverse both Afghanistan and Pakistan, thereby putting the pipeline at risk due to instability in Afghanistan and giving Pakistan the ability to threaten India's access to energy. However, recent positive trends in relations between India and Pakistan have improved the feasibility of this plan.

The Central Asian countries also provide a convenient and low-cost hub for Indian travelers. Services in the form of flights from India to London, the United States, and Europe provide a lucrative export for Uzbekistan. However, for commodity trade in other areas,

---

[21] Interfax-Kazakhstan News Agency (2005b); Federation of Indian Chambers of Commerce and Industry (n.d.).

[22] Indian Embassy in Turkmenistan (2004).

[23] Author interviews with Indian Embassy officials and specialists in Central Asia, summer 2003.

[24] Fact sheet received from Indian Embassy officials in Turkmenistan, summer 2003.

Indian businesspeople note that currency conversion restrictions mean that repatriation of profits is a problem, hampering the expansion of economic ties.[25]

The U.S. Role

India views a continued role for the United States in the region as positive for its interests. The continued existence of terrorist groups and drug trafficking in Afghanistan and Pakistan remains a primary concern for India, and it seeks help from the United States in stabilizing Afghanistan and securing the region against terrorist groups. To date, there has been little clear cooperation in Central Asia between the United States and India, and this may be an area in which to explore the possibility of greater coordination. Cooperation could draw upon common interests in the region in countering terrorist groups, stemming drug trafficking, and promoting democracy and stability.

---

[25] Author interviews with Indian business executives in Central Asia, summer 2003.

CHAPTER SEVEN

Conclusions: Implications for U.S. Interests

The Asian countries bordering Central Asia have distinct and growing interests in the region. For most states, regional security and economic ties form the central issues of interest. Trade across the region, in the energy sector and otherwise, is difficult if not impossible without stability and development. Regional organizations such as the SCO could have a role in promoting these common objectives. However, not all of the interested parties have the same perspective or approach to addressing regional security, weakening the effectiveness of organizations such as the SCO.

China would like to have broader influence in Central Asia, both economically and in security matters. Trade is growing rapidly between China and the states of Central Asia, and China is pursuing energy ties aggressively. Concerns regarding Uighur separatists have driven China to support aggressive policies against militants and to develop cooperative security relationships with the Central Asian states. Chinese apprehension regarding U.S. presence in Central Asia provides yet more incentives for China to strengthen regional security cooperation through the SCO.

India also seeks to build a relationship with the Central Asian states, but its security focus in doing so has far more to do with counterterrorism efforts than with seeking local hegemony. India's concerns revolve around the possible resurgence of the Taliban and other militant groups that pose a direct security threat. As most transport routes to the region traverse Afghanistan, for India, a stable Afghanistan is also critical to expanding economic ties with Central Asia. In contrast, Pakistan remains a smaller player in Central Asia, as suspicion toward its role in supporting regional Islamic militants remains throughout the region. Nonetheless, Pakistan is working toward greater economic ties with the region.

Iran's interests are largely economic in nature. While it, like India, China, and Russia, has been building security relationships with these countries, Iran's primary focus now appears to be in expanding trade, transport, and energy links with the region. A stable Afghanistan is required for Iran to have a productive relationship with the region. However, Iran also has concerns that U.S. military presence in the region could be aimed at containing Iran, or worse.

Friends, allies, and others have watched the recent development of U.S. security ties with the Central Asian states with significant concern and some trepidation. All are curious if the United States does, indeed, intend a long-term presence in the region, and wonder not only what this means for the region's future, but also what it indicates about U.S. global policy.

Thus, U.S. actions have enormous potential to shape the future of foreign involvement. While other neighbors and interested parties are concerned about U.S. "neo-imperialism," they also recognize that the United States can deliver more of the stability everyone seeks for the region than can any other actor. The question is whether it plans to take on that role, and, if so, with what long-term purpose in mind. The solution may well be that the United States must lead with transparency and cooperation, working with India and China (and even, insofar as it is possible, Iran) so as to better leverage and better understand the efforts of others. This would also serve to assuage some aspects of concern in Asia about U.S. policies and it would help demonstrate to the countries of Central Asia that seeking the United States as a patron is far less effective than building friendly and balanced ties with a broad range of interested nations.

Bibliography

Anis, "Afghan Paper Condemns Pakistan's Pro-Fundamentalist Bias," *BBC Worldwide Monitoring: International Reports*, March 11, 2003.

"Armitage Visits President Musharraf at Army Headquarters: Pakistani Official," *Agence France Presse*, October 6, 2003.

Asia-Plus News Agency, "Iran, China Help Tajikistan Modernize Telephone System," *BBC Worldwide Monitoring: International Reports*, July 15, 2003a.

————, "Iran Set to Give Tajikistan 31 Million Dollars in Aid, Credit," *BBC Worldwide Monitoring: International Reports*, July 16, 2003b.

————, "Tajikistan Sends Cadets to India for Training," *BBC Worldwide Monitoring: International Reports*, March 3, 2003c.

Associated Press of Pakistan, "Pakistan Arrests Five Terror Suspects, Four Said from Uzbekistan," *BBC Worldwide Monitoring: International Reports*, August 24, 2004.

Avesta, "Road Linking Tajikistan, Afghanistan, Iran To Be Built Soon," *BBC Worldwide Monitoring: International Reports*, September 8, 2004.

Baker, Peter, "Renewed Militancy Seen in Uzbekistan; Government Crackdown Threatens to Radicalize Previously Non-Violent Groups," *Washington Post*, September 27, 2003, p. A19.

Bedi, Rahul, "India and Central Asia," *Frontline*, Vol. 19, Issue 19, September 14–27, 2002.

Burghart, Daniel L., and Theresa Sabonis-Helf, eds., *In the Tracks of Tamerlane: Central Asia's Path to the 21st Century*, National Defense

University Center for Technology and National Security Policy, Washington, D.C.: U.S. Government Printing Office, 2004.

Burles, Mark, *Chinese Policy Toward Russia and the Central Asian Republics,* Santa Monica, Calif.: RAND Corporation, MR-1045-AF, 1999. Online at http://www.rand.org/publications/MR/MR1045 (as of November 14, 2005).

"China: Formation of Regional Antiterrorist Agency in Central Asia Completed," *Kyrgyz-Press International News Agency,* April 1, 2003.

"China Grants No-Strings Aid to Uzbekistan," *BBC Worldwide Monitoring: International Reports,* February 15, 2003.

"China Keeps Wary Eye on Kyrgyzstan Revolution," *Asia Pulse,* April 5, 2005.

"China, Russia, Central Asian Nations Begin Antiterror Drills," *Kyodo News Service,* August 6, 2003.

"China's Trade with Uzbekistan in January 2005," *Xinhua News Agency,* March 18, 2005.

"Chinese Traders Await Long-Term Stability in Kyrgyzstan," *AFX-Asia,* March 29, 2005.

"Delhi Tracks Al Qaeda, Jaish Links," *Gulf News,* October 11, 2001.

"Different Views on Anti-Terrorist Operation in Afghanistan at Kazakh Round Table," *Interfax-Kazakhstan News Agency,* September 11, 2002.

Federation of Indian Chambers of Commerce and Industry, "India-Kazakh Commercial Relations," no date. Online at http://www.ficci.com/ficci/international/countries/Kazakhstan/kazakhstancommercialrelation.htm (as of May 11, 2005).

Gall, Carlotta, "In Pakistan Border Towns, Taliban Has a Resurgence," *New York Times,* May 6, 2003, p. 21.

George, Paul, "Country Perspectives China: Islamic Unrest in the Xinjiang Uighur Autonomous Region," Commentary No. 73, Canadian Security Service Publication, 1998.

Gill, Bates, and Matthew Oresman, *China's New Journey to the West: China's Emergence in Central Asia and Implications for U.S. Interests,* Washington, D.C.: Center for Strategic and International Studies (CSIS), 2003.

"Great Gamer India Sets Up First Overseas Base," *India Business Insight*, September 8, 2002.

Haniffa, Aziz, "India to Have Access to U.S. Intelligence," *The Times of India*, October 8, 2000.

Hyman, Anthony, "Russia, Central Asia, and the Taliban," in William Maley, ed., *Fundamentalism Reborn? Afghanistan and the Taliban*, New York: New York University Press, 2001.

Ibraimov, Bakyt, "Uighurs: Beijing to Blame for Kyrgyz Crackdown," *Eurasianet.org*, January 28, 2004.

"India, Tajikistan to Intensify Defence Cooperation," *The Press Trust of India*, November 14, 2003.

"India, Uzbekistan Sign Pacts on Defense, Trade," *Asia Pulse*, April 7, 2005.

"India, Uzbekistan Vow to Fight Terrorism, Sign 12 Accords," *The Press Trust of India*, April 5, 2005.

Indian Embassy in Turkmenistan, 2004. Online at http://meaindia.nic.in/foreignrelation/trkmenistan.htm (as of May 11, 2005).

Interfax News Agency, "Uighur Separatists May Be Involved in Terrorism in Kyrgyzstan," *BBC Worldwide Monitoring: International Reports*, May 23, 2003.

———, "New Kyrgyz Authorities Anxious to Maintain Investment, Specialists," *BBC Worldwide Monitoring: International Reports*, March 31, 2005.

Interfax-Kazakhstan News Agency, "Wounded Kazakh Diplomat Dies in Pakistan," *BBC Worldwide Monitoring: International Reports*, January 21, 2005a.

———, "Kazakhstan, India Set to Develop Cooperation in Oil, Gas Sector," *BBC Worldwide Monitoring: International Reports*, February 17, 2005b.

"Iran Supplying Arms to Anti-Taleban Forces Through Tajikistan," *Deutsche Presse-Agentur*, January 10, 1999.

"Iran to Keep Troops on Afghanistan Border Until Security Ensured," *Deutsche Presse-Agentur*, September 24, 1998.

"Iran, Turkmenistan Inaugurate 'Dam of Friendship' on Border," *Deutsche Presse-Agentur*, April 12, 2005.

"Iran, Uzbekistan, Afghanistan to Expand Transportation Cooperation," *BBC Worldwide Monitoring: International Reports*, November 22, 2004.

IRNA—see Islamic Republic News Agency.

Islamic Republic News Agency, "Iran, Kyrgyzstan Discuss Energy Cooperation," *BBC Worldwide Monitoring: International Reports*, September 21, 2004a.

———, "Iran, Kazakhstan Underline Regional Security Cooperation," *BBC Worldwide Monitoring: International Reports*, October 11, 2004b.

———, "Iran: Khatami Says No Foreign Troops Needed for Caucasus, Central Asia Security," *BBC Worldwide Monitoring International Reports*, January 1, 2005a.

———, "Iran Vice President Calls for Expansion of Economic Ties with Uzbekistan," *BBC Worldwide Monitoring: International Reports*, January 5, 2005b.

———, "Iran, Tajikistan Sign Consular Document," *BBC Worldwide Monitoring: International Reports*, March 4, 2005c.

ITAR-TASS News Agency, "Kyrgyz Minister Says Terrorists May Infiltrate Central Asia from Afghanistan," *BBC Worldwide Monitoring: International Reports*, August 2, 2002.

Kabar News Agency, "Two Wanted for Kyrgyz Bus Attack Identified as Chinese," *BBC Worldwide Monitoring: International Reports*, October 18, 2004.

Kaplan, Robert D., "The Lawless Frontier," *The Atlantic Monthly*, Vol. 286, No. 3, 2000, pp. 66–80.

Karavan, "Kazakhstan's Uighur Separatists Seen as 'Trump Card' against China," *BBC Worldwide Monitoring: International Reports*, December 2, 2002.

"Kazakhstan Keen to Boost Trade Ties with Iran," *Asia Pulse*, April 7, 2005.

"Kazakhstan to Build Two Oil Terminals in Iran," *Asia Pulse*, June 21, 2004.

Kazakhstanskaya Pravda, "Kazakh Oil to Be Shipped to China Via New Pipeline in May 2006," *BBC Worldwide Monitoring: International Reports*, February 12, 2005.

Kozlova, Marina, "Kyrgyzstan Dances with U.S., China," *United Press International*, October 10, 2002.

———, "Fleeing Uzbek Rebels Escaped to Pakistan," *United Press International*, February 27, 2003.

Kyrgyz AKI Press, "Kyrgyzstan Backs India, Pakistan Entry into Shanghai Organization," *BBC Worldwide Monitoring: International Reports*, December 18, 2003.

Kyrgyz Television, "Kyrgyzstan Voices Concern Over 'Record Poppy Harvest' in Afghanistan," *BBC Worldwide Monitoring: International Reports*, February 11, 2005.

Kyrgyz Television First Channel, "Iran To Give 1 Million Dollars in Aid to Kyrgyzstan," *BBC Worldwide Monitoring: International Reports*, June 21, 2004a.

———, "Kyrgyzstan, China Sign Electricity Accord," *BBC Worldwide Monitoring: International Reports*, November 17, 2004b.

"'Made in Pakistan' Exhibition Begins in Tajikistan," *Business Recorder*, April 29, 2005.

Meyer, Henry, "India and Russia Find Common Ground over Afghan Threat," *Agence France Presse*, October 5, 2000.

"Now, India Makes a Beeline for Kazakh Oil," *Hindustan Times*, February 18, 2005.

Oliker, Olga, and David A. Shlapak, *U.S. Interests in Central Asia: Policy Priorities and Military Roles*, Santa Monica, Calif: RAND Corporation, MG-338-AF, 2005. Online at http://rand.org/publications/MG/MG338 (as of November 14, 2005).

"Pak Police Identifies IA Hijacker as Suspect in Pearl Case," *The Press Trust of India*, February 15, 2002.

"Pakistan and Uzbekistan Vow to Intensify Efforts Against Terrorism," *The Pakistan Newswire*, March 6, 2005.

"Pakistan Finds 'Unacceptable' U.S. Military Incursions," *Channel NewsAsia*, May 24, 2004.

"Pakistan-Kyrgyzstan Sign Agreements, Vow to Expand Bilateral Trade," *The Pakistan Newswire*, March 7, 2005.

"Pakistan Protests U.S. Troops Firing in South Waziristan," *Pakistan Press International*, January 3, 2005.

"Pakistan Signs MOU with Tajikistan to Buy Power," *Asia Pulse*, April 4, 2005.

"Pamphlets Urging Attacks on U.S. Troops Handed Out in Pakistani Mosques," *Agence France Presse*, January 31, 2003.

"President Karzai Announces New Afghan Cabinet," *Deutsche Presse-Agentur*, December 23, 2004.

Pakistan Television Corporation, "Pakistan, Afghanistan, Turkmenistan Sign Gas Pipeline Protocol," *BBC Worldwide Monitoring: International Reports*, April 13, 2005.

Pakistan Television Corporation World, "Pakistan President Keen to Promote Economic, Political Ties with Uzbekistan," *BBC Worldwide Monitoring: International Reports*, March 7, 2005.

PTV—see Pakistan Television Corporation.

Rahman, Shaikh Azizur, "India Strikes for Oil and Gas with Military Base in Tajikistan," *Washington Times*, September 2, 2002, p. A1.

Rashid, Ahmed, *Taliban: Militant Islam, Oil, and Fundamentalism in Central Asia*, New Haven, Conn.: Yale University Press, 2000.

———, "Pakistan and the Taliban," in William Maley, ed., *Fundamentalism Reborn? Afghanistan and the Taliban*, New York: New York University Press, 2001.

———, *Jihad: The Rise of Militant Islam in Central Asia*, New Haven, Conn.: Yale University, 2002.

Rohde, David, "Pakistan: Attack Plotters Caught, Police Say," *New York Times*, August 24, 2002, p. 6.

Shah, Amir, "Warlord Accuses Rival of Breaking Spirit of Ceasefire," *The Associated Press*, August 23, 2004.

"Tajik-India," *The Press Trust of India*, July 8, 2003.

Tajik Television, "Iran to Give 5M Dollars for Tajik Road Project," *BBC Worldwide Monitoring: International Reports*, September 14, 2004.

————, "Tajikistan, Russia, Iran Strike Deal on Power Plant Construction," *BBC Worldwide Monitoring: International Reports*, January 12, 2005.

Tajik Television First Channel, "Tajik Leader, U.N. Envoy Discuss Relations, Regional Issues, Afghanistan," *BBC Worldwide Monitoring: International Reports*, October 18, 2002.

"Tajikistan: Iran Allocates Total of $30 Million for Tunnel, Economic Projects," *Infoprod*, May 27, 2003.

"Tajikistan, Kazakhstan Endorse India's Bid for Seat in UNSC," *Hindustan Times*, May 9, 2005.

"Tajikistan Welcomes India Joining Shanghai's Club," *ITAR-TASS*, November 13, 2003.

"Talks Held on Turkmenistan-Afghanistan-Pakistan Gas Pipeline," *Asia Pulse*, April 13, 2005.

Turkmen Government, "Turkmenistan Opens Second Power Transmission Line to Iran," *BBC Worldwide Monitoring: International Reports*, August 23, 2004.

Usaeva, Nadia, "Kyrgyzstan: Trial Focuses Attention on Possible Uighur Repression," *Radio Free Europe/Radio Liberty*, August 31, 2001.

"Uzbek, Iranian Businesses, Officials Meet in Uzbekistan," *UzReport.com*, March 11, 2005.

"Uzbekistan President Starts State Visit to India," *Asia Pulse*, April 5, 2005.

Uzbek Radio, "India to Get Six Tanker Aircraft from Uzbekistan by End 2003," *BBC Worldwide Monitoring: International Reports*, March 1, 2003.

Uzbek Television, "Deal Giving Uzbekistan Access to Iranian Coasts Via Afghanistan Signed," *BBC Worldwide Monitoring: International Reports*, January 5, 2005.

Uzbek Television Second Channel, "Uzbekistan, China Sign Economic, Cultural, Partnership Accords," *BBC Worldwide Monitoring: International Reports*, June 16, 2004.

"Uzbekistan Seeks Information about Militants Arrested in Pakistan," *The Pakistan Newswire*, April 3, 2004.

Vecherniy Bishkek, "Kyrgyz Paper Sees Religious Organization as Terrorist Trojan Horse," *BBC Worldwide Monitoring: International Reports*, October 28, 2002.

Vision of the Islamic Republic of Iran Network 1, "Iran–Turkmenistan Friendship Dam Officially Operational," *BBC Worldwide Monitoring: International Reports*, April 10, 2004.

Voice of the Islamic Republic of Iran, "Tajikistan Sets up Anti-Drug Agency in Afghanistan," *BBC Worldwide Monitoring: International Reports*, January 15, 2005.

Wright, Robin, and Ann Scott Tyson, "U.S. Evicted from Air Base in Uzbekistan," *Washington Post*, July 30, 2005, p. A1.